Ruiliang Yan

Internet Retailing

I0009649

Ruiliang Yan

Internet Retailing

Pricing, Product and Information Strategies

VDM Verlag Dr. Müller

ISBN: 978-3-8364-1487-6

PRICING AND INFORMATION STRATEGIES ON THE INTERNET RETAILING

Abstract

This book includes three business scenarios addressing the value of market information and pricing strategies in the Internet retailing.

First, we study the product choice and the value of information accuracy for the online retailers in the chapter one. The focus of this study is information forecast value and the profound impact it has in today's business market. When a retailer sells its product through the Internet-based market, the value of market information has an important impact on its expected profit. The value of market information depends not only on its accuracy but also on the product characteristics the retailer sells. We develop a theoretic approach to examine how the effect of market information on firm profit is moderated by product characteristics. Our results suggest that more accurate market information always is more valuable for firm profit when product quality is higher and product web-fit is larger. Based on our analytical results, we propose the optimal marketing strategies for the online retailers to adopt.

Second, we study the marketing information and dual-channel pricing strategies in a multi-channel retailer in the chapter two. With the rapid development of the Internet, many manufacturers nowadays use this technology to engage in direct sales. The mix of retailing with a direct channel adds a new dimension of competition and complementarities to a product's distribution channels. An important strategic issue, for managers planning to use a mixed online and traditional retail channel, is the pricing strategy. To determine the right pricing strategy, we develop a game theoretical model that allows for competition between the dual-channel stores. We demonstrate that optimal pricing strategy exists under either the Bertrand competition or the integrated settings with demand certainty and uncertainty in a mixed online and traditional retail channel. When the demand is certain, the optimal pricing strategy for online and traditional channels to adopt is to use a low-high pricing strategy. However, when the demand is uncertain, the forecast accuracy strategically impacts on the setting of pricing strategy for online and traditional retail channels and further impacts on the profits of dual-channel stores. We further show that information accuracy always is more valuable to the traditional channel store under all types of market structures. Based on our results, we propose appropriate strategies for business managers who are using or planning to use a mixed channel to sell their products.

Finally, we investigate the value of information sharing in a manufacturer-ecommerce retailer supply chain in the chapter three. The value of market information depends not only on its accuracy but also on the e-retailer's market power and the product's web compatibility. We develop a theoretical approach to examine the value of information sharing for the manufacturer and the e-retailer first, and then we further check to see how information sharing is moderated by the e-retailer's market share and the product's e-market base demand. Our results suggest that under some conditions, both the manufacturer and the e-retailer can be better off from information sharing. Especially when the e-retailer's market share is larger and the product's e-market base demand is higher, the information sharing is more valuable for the supply chain players. Using our analysis findings, we indicate marketing strategies

that the manufacturer and the e-retailer may want to adopt.

TABLE OF CONTENTS

LIST OF FIGURES

LIST OF TABLES

CHAPTER ONE

PRODUCT CHOICE AND INFORMATION STRATEGIES FOR ONLINE

RETAILERS

1.1. Introduction

The advent of Internet-based electronic commerce over the past decade has given businesses an unprecedented marketing opportunity. According to Comscore Networks, online retail spending in 2006 reached $102.1 billion, marking a 24 percent increase over 2005's $82.3 billion. An estimated 6 percent of all non-travel consumer retail spending (excluding expenditures for autos, gasoline, and food) is spent online. Also, according to Forrester Research, European e-commerce is forecasted to surge to €263 billion in 2011, with travel, clothes, groceries, and consumer electronics all reaching the €10 billion per year mark. As a result, the rapid development of commerce on the Internet has made it attractive for retailers or individuals to engage in direct online sales, especially for those products that are more suitable for selling through the online market. With the rapid development of ecommerce, information is becoming more and more important in improving firm's performance. Information, when available, is often difficult to resist, and it is not surprising that there is an increasing trend towards acquiring more sophisticated and detailed information about the market.

Our research examines how product characteristics affect the value of information. While information can be of many different types, we focus on information that can help reduce uncertainty about future demand. The retailers can use the accurate information to response to customer demand more quickly. There is obviously no doubt that a good information base helps decision making. Some of the questions addressed in our research can be summarized as follows.

1. Does the same improvement in information precision have a larger or lower impact on the profit of online retailer when the product quality is higher?

2. Does the same improvement in information precision have a larger or lower impact on the profit of online retailer when the web-product fit is larger?

3. Does the same improvement in information precision have a larger or lower impact on the profit of online retailer when customers' preference for product quality is higher?

Our findings may be relevant for providers of information by helping them identify the value of information. The qualitative insights from our research may also be useful for retailers planning on how to improve market information precision, which then get transmitted to firm profits. The online retailers can use the insights from our research to effectively allocate financial resources on improving information precision, especially when the product quality is higher and the product is more suitable for selling through the online market.

The remainder of our paper is organized as follows. Section 2 discusses relevant literature. Section 3 presents our modeling for online retailers. Section 4 analyzes the value of market information on online retailer's expected profit, and how it will be affected by product quality, product web-fit and the customers' preference

for product quality, respectively. In the section 5, we illustrate our important findings

about the value of market information for online retailer by means of simulation

examples. A summary of key results and managerial insights are presented in the

section 6. All relevant proofs are relegated to the Appendix for clarity of exposition.

1.2. Literature Review

Given the increasing importance of information, researchers have looked at

the subject of information from a variety of perspectives. Raju and Roy (2000)

provide a good summary of this by discussing the studies done by, among others,

Hilton (1981), Vives (1984), Morrison and Schmittlein (1991), Blattberg and Hoch

(1990), Padmanabhan and Rao (1993), Day (1990), Glazer (1991), Sarvary and Parker

(1997). Raju and Roy (2000) themselves examined the impact of market information

on firm performance. Their results showed that information is always more valuable

in more competitive industries and for larger firms. Gavirneni, Kapuscinski and Tayur

(1999) studied partial and complete shared information of inventory policies between

a supplier and a retailer, and they estimated the savings of the supplier due to

information sharing and addressed when information sharing was more valuable.

Cachon and Fisher (2000) investigated the value of information sharing between one

supplier and multiple identical retailers. They found that information sharing led to

substantial savings from lead time and batch size reduction. Lee, So and Tang (2000)

studied the value of information sharing in a two level supply chain and found that information sharing can provide significant inventory reduction and cost saving. Raju and Roy (2000) examined the impact of market information on the firm performance. Their results showed that information always is more valuable in more competitive industries and for larger firms. Corbett, Zhou and Tang (2004) studied the value to a supplier of obtaining better information about a buyer's cost structure and of being able to offer more general contracts. They found that the value of information is higher under two-part contacts and the value of offerings two-part contracts is higher under full information. Mishra and Prasad (2004) showed that it is more profitable for the firm to delegate pricing authority to the sales-force with private information.

However, no prior research about market information so far has been directly done on online market with product characteristics. Our paper addresses these limitations in current research by studying the value of market information in an online market jointly with the effect of product characteristics when the retailers or individuals engage in online direct sales.

In this paper, we consider a single product sold through online market, where the customers' preference for product quality is uncertain. Online retailer uses information precision to reduce the uncertainty. First, we obtain the optimal price policy and the corresponding expected profit. And then we study how the value of market information on the firm profit is moderated by product quality, product web-fit, and the customers' preference for product quality, respectively. Based on our results, we propose the optimal marketing strategies for the retailers or individuals to adopt when they plan to engage in online direct sales.

1.3. Model Framework

In this section, we assume a monopoly market where there is no channel competition. We introduce the basic demand model and the channel pricing decision when a product is sold through an online market. The schematic representation of this Internet channel model is shown in figure 1.1.

Insert in Figure 1.1 here

Product quality is worth q when this product is inspected on the spot and customer can possess it immediately. However, the online product could face a chance of being delivered late without immediate possession and is short of touch, taste, smell and real evaluation. As a result, the perceived product quality is only worth θq ($0 < \theta \leq 1$) in the online market. There is a substantial body of literature (e.g., Chiang et al., 1998), which indicates that when the same product is purchased on the Internet, it is of less value to the consumer. Liang and Huang (1998) did an empirical study to show that customers prefer traditional markets more than direct markets. Kacen et al. (2002) also show that customer acceptance of web-based purchases, based on empirical analysis of data, turns out to be less than one for many product categories (Table 1.1).

Insert in Table 1.1 here

There can be several reasons for why consumers perceive identical products purchased on the web to be less valuable as compared to when they are bought in a traditional channel. One reason could be that many of the product attributes that are transparent to a consumer in a traditional channel, such as the fit of a pair of trousers, are hidden on the web. Another reason might be that on the web, gratification is delayed, whereas it is instant in the retail channel. It is also difficult to return products on the web. We call this factor product web-fit, θ, and $0 < \theta \leq 1$.

Customers are assumed to be heterogeneous in their willingness to pay for product quality. The customers' preference for product quality is described by an index R with an assumption of normal distribution. A product sold online for price p is perceived to be of quality of θq, thus when the customer buys this product, the utility function is $u = R\theta q - p$. The customer will buy this product provided he can only derive positive utility. Otherwise, he will not buy it. Thus, the marginal consumer whose valuation R^d equals $p/\theta q$ is indifferent to buying from the online market. If $R > R^d$, customers prefer to buy from the online market. Given above analysis, the firm's demand function is

$$d(p,q,\theta) = R - \frac{p}{\theta q} \tag{1}$$

1.3.1. Uncertainty Modeling

Insert in Figure 1.2 here

To capture uncertainty in market demand resulting from heterogeneous consumers in their willing to pay for product quality, we assume that R, the customers' preference for product quality, is a random variable. Specifically, we assume that $R = \overline{R} + e$, where e is assumed to be normal distribution with mean zero and variance τ_q, that is $\text{var}(R - \overline{R}) = \tau_q$. Although the normality assumption has its limitations in negative values, we assume that $\overline{R}$ is large, relative to τ_q, so that the probability of negative demand is negligible. As in Vives (1984), we confine the demand uncertainty to additive intercept term. Using its own market-information-gathering techniques at its disposal, the firm makes a forecast about customers' preference for product quality. Firm's forecast of the customers' preference for product quality in the online market is s. We assume that

$$s = R + \varepsilon \tag{2}$$

Where $\varepsilon \sim N(0, \sigma)$, and is independent of the customers' preference for product quality, R. Forecasts can range from perfect ($\sigma = 0$ or infinite precision) to pure noise ($\sigma = \infty$ or zero precision) The precision of forecast is given σ, which also represents the market information accuracy. Market information is more accurate when σ is smaller. Under the normality assumption (as well as the generalized linear information structure) conditional expectation are linear. We have that

$$E(R \mid s) = (1 - t)\overline{R} + ts \tag{3}$$

Where, $t = \dfrac{\tau_q}{\sigma + \tau_q}$ (Cyert and DeGroot, 1970, 1973; Vives, 1984). As σ ranges

from ∞ to 0, the forecast goes from being perfectly informative to being not

informative at all and at the same time t ranges from 1 to 0. When the information is

perfect, $E(R \mid s) = s$; when there is no information, $E(R \mid s) = \overline{R}$

The proposed model structure also suggests that

$$E[(s - \overline{R})^2] = \tau_q + \sigma \qquad (4)$$

We assume that the firm maximizes its expected profit by choosing optimal

pricing policy. Thus the expected profit, conditional on the forecast of customers'

preference for product quality, can be expressed as follows.

$$E(\pi \mid s) = p[E(R - \dfrac{p}{\theta q}) \mid s)] \qquad (5)$$

Where π is the profit from online market sales; p is the abbreviated forms of $p(s)$.

1.4. Equilibrium Analysis

First, we drive the equilibrium price and expected profit. Then we examine

how the effect of market information on firm's expected profit is moderated by the

different parameters.

1.4.1. Equilibrium price and profit

The equilibrium price policy and expected profit are summarized as follows:

$$p = \frac{q\theta\overline{R}}{2} + \frac{q\theta}{2}t(s - \overline{R}) \qquad (6)$$

$$E[\pi] = \frac{q\theta((\sigma + \tau_q)t^2 + \overline{R}^2)}{4} \qquad (7)$$

If there is no uncertainty ($\tau_q = 0$), the equilibrium price for online retailer would have

been $p = \dfrac{q\theta\overline{R}}{2}$ and the expected profit would be $E[\pi] = \dfrac{q\theta\overline{R}^2}{4}$.

Now we consider the more general case in which the consumers' preference for product quality is uncertain, firm makes forecast of consumers' preference for product quality and includes this forecast information in its pricing policy. If the forecast is completely uninformative ($\sigma = \infty$, which is $t \approx 0$), then the firm will not use its forecast and use only the prior mean $\overline{R}$. The equilibrium price is $p = \dfrac{q\theta\overline{R}}{2}$,

and the expected profit will be $E[\pi] = \dfrac{q\theta\overline{R}^2}{4}$. If the forecast is perfectly accurate

($\sigma = 0$, which is $t \approx 1$), then the firm will not depend on the prior mean $\overline{R}$ and use only its forecast. The equilibrium price is $p = \dfrac{sq\theta}{2}$, and the expected profit will

be $E[\pi] = \dfrac{s^2q\theta}{4}$. However, at the most of time, when the forecast is not perfect

($0 < t < 1$), the equilibrium price will be a combination of prior mean $\overline{R}$ and forecast s, and the expected profit will be a combination of prior mean $\overline{R}$ and forecast precision σ.

1.4.2. Consumers' preference uncertainty

Because $t = \dfrac{\tau_q}{\sigma + \tau_q}$, thus equation (7) can be rewritten as follows.

$$E[\pi] = \frac{1}{4} q \theta \overline{R}^2 + \frac{q \theta \tau_q^2}{4(\sigma + \tau_q)} \qquad (8)$$

First, we differentiate the equation (8) with respect to τ_q, and furthermore, we differentiate $\dfrac{\partial E[\pi]}{\partial \tau_q}$ with respect to θ, then we obtain the proposition 1.

Proposition 1: *The online retailer's expected profit increases with the consumers' preference uncertainty, especially when the web-product fit is larger.*

Proof. Proof is in Appendix 1.

Proposition suggests that the online retailer always benefits from larger market demand uncertainty. As the market is more volatile, the online retailer would enjoy increasing profit. Especially when the product is more compatible to online market, the online retailer profits much more. The rationale is that when uncertain increases, the larger profits resulting from very high primary demand dominate the smaller profits resulting from a very low primary demand (the mean keeps the same).

1.4.3. Value of market information

By differentiating equation (8) with respect to σ, we find that the online retailer's profit always increases with the information precision. This result is consistent with Vives's (1984) finding that the private value of information precision to firms always is positive.

1.4.3.1. Effect of web-product fit on the value of market information

Furthermore, in order to examine the effect of web-product fit on the value of market information, we differentiate $\frac{\partial E[\pi]}{\partial \sigma}$ with respect to θ. Since $\frac{\partial E[\pi]}{\partial \sigma}$ measures the effect of a change in market information on online retailer's expected profit, consequently, $(\partial(\frac{\partial E[\pi]}{\partial \sigma})/\partial \theta)$ effectively measures how the link between market information and online retailer's expected profit is moderated by the web-product fit. Therefore, from our analysis, we come up with proposition 2 as follows.

Proposition 2: *The effect of a change in the market information on the online retailer's expected profit always increases with the web-product fit, θ.*

Proof. Proof is given in Appendix 2

The values of θ reflect the competitive advantage in a product market. When the value of θ is larger or the product is more compatible with online market, higher precise market information will bring much more profit to online retailer. This result is consistent with the finding in McGee and Prusak (1993) that accurate information is more important in a competitive market.

1.4.3.2. Effect of product quality on the value of market information

In order to examine the effect of product quality on the value of market information, we differentiate $\frac{\partial E[\pi]}{\partial \sigma}$ with respect to q and obtain proposition 3.

Proposition 3: *The effect of a change in the market information on the online retailer's expected profit always increases with the product quality, q.*

Proof. Proof is given in Appendix 3

Similarly, to the extant that the product quality also reflects the degree of competitive advantage in a product market, if the product quality is higher, the market information precision will be much more valuable for the online retailer.

1.4.3.3. Effect of consumers' preference on the value of market information

In order to examine the effect of customers' preference for product quality on the value of market information, we differentiate $\dfrac{\partial E[\pi]}{\partial \sigma}$ with respect to $\bar{R}$. We obtain the following proposition 4.

Proposition 4: *The effect of a change in market information on online retailer's expected profit is not affected by consumers' preference for product quality, $\bar{R}$.*

In the context of our model, it turns out that the value of market information is not affected by the consumers' preference for product quality, $\bar{R}$. This could be potentially contrary to the common belief that higher consumers' preference for product quality should have a larger impact on the value of market information. The reason is that our normality assumption might drive this result because the mean and variance in normal distribution are independent. It is interesting in future research to examine the impact of consumers' preference for product quality on the value of market information by the empirical study.

1.5. Illustrative Simulation Examples

While our findings in propositions can be derived analytically, the analytical expressions are too complex to provide meaningful insights. Thus we now present simulation examples to illustrate the impact of model parameter σ on online retailer's expected profits, and further indicate how the model parameters θ and q impact on the value of market information. The values we use for the various parameters are shown in Table 1.2 and we always vary the values of σ from 0 to 0.1. Our intention is to examine the strategic effect of market information on online retailer. We vary some of the parameters to find their effect on the optimum policies. We simulate 100*100 trials – a total of 1 million trials each run. This brought the standard deviation of our expected profit estimate to within 1% of the mean. For each set of parameters analyzed, we determined the online retailer' expected profits.

Insert in Figure 1.3 here

Figure 1.3 shows that retailer always can benefit from accurate market information. The more accurate the market information is, the larger the online retailer's expected profit is.

Insert in Figure 1.4 here

Next, we plot a three dimension graph to illustrate the effect of product web-fit on the value of market information. Here we vary the value of θ from 0 to 1 to investigate the effect of product web-fit on the value of market information when the values of σ vary from 0 to 0.1. Figure 1.4 shows that the online retailer's expected profit is continuously increasing with the values of σ when the values of θ increase.

Insert in Figure 1.5 here

Finally, we plot another three dimension graph to illustrate the effect of product quality on the value of market information. Similarly, we vary the value of q from 1 to 10 to investigate the effect of product quality on the value of market information when the values of σ vary from 0 to 0.1. Figure 1.5 shows that the online retailer's expected profit is continuously increasing with the values of σ when the values of q increase.

To ascertain optimal marketing strategies for the online retailer, we study the above Figures in conjunction. When the retailers engage in direct sales through online market, they will be motivated to improve the accuracy of market information. Any more accurate market information will contribute to improve the online retailer's expected profits. Especially, when the product categories are more compatible to online market or product quality is higher, the market information will be much more valuable to the online retailer.

1.6. Conclusions and Managerial Implications

The contributions of this study are both theoretical and substantive in nature. Our focus in this paper is on the value of market information and the profound impact it plays on the expected profit of online retailer. In this paper, we provide a theoretical framework for studying the strategic value of market information in an online market and further examine how the value of market information is moderated by product quality, product web-fit, and the consumers' preference for product quality, respectively. We summarize the results in the following table.

Insert in Table 1.3 here

Our results indicate that more accurate market information is always more valuable for firm profit when the product web-fit is larger and the product quality is higher. These results provide important insights for business online managers. For instance, Amazon, overstock, and other online firms, they may need direct more financial resources for acquiring higher precise market information when the product is more compatible to online market and the product quality is higher.

Since the Internet channel is booming on sales, it is managerially important to develop a mechanism of improving the accuracy of market information. This is an intuition based conclusion. In our paper, we use mathematical models to show that this intuition can be made objective by using a Bayesian forecasting mechanism. We prove that by strategically improving the accuracy of market information forecast, the online retailer can effectively improve its overall profit. Especially, when the product is more compatible to online market and the product quality is higher, online retailer benefits much more from the higher precise market information.

This finding is of immense managerial significance since the online retailer knowing that its profits would be enhanced, would do its best to improve the market information. Our research shows that in the business world, there is a need for online retailer to appreciate the ramifications of a well-planned information-improving strategy. For instance, online retailer can adopt the strategy of information sharing to improve the accuracy of market information.

Table 1.1: Product acceptance index θ for web-based online market

Category	Book	Shoes	Toothpaste	DVD player	Flowers	Food items
Acceptance	0.904	0.769	0.886	0.787	0.792	0.784

Note: All product categories have θ below 1.0 at the 1% significance level

Table 1.2: Market and product Characteristics

Parameters	Base value and (range of values)
$\overline{R}$	8 (1-10)
θ	0.8 (0-1)
q	8 (1-10)
τ_q	0.05 (0-0.1)

Table 1.3: Summarized findings

Effect of	On the value of market information
Larger product web-fit θ	Greater
Higher product quality q	Greater
Higher consumers' preference $\overline{R}$	No Effect

Figure 1.1: The Internet channel diagram

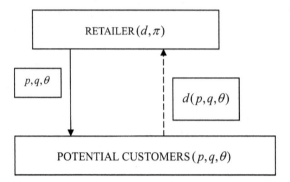

The following is the definition of the symbols that appear in Figure 1.1.

π : Online retailer's profit

d : Demand of the online market

p : Price in the online market

q : Denotes product quality

θ : Denotes product web-fit

Figure 1.2: The information forecast diagram

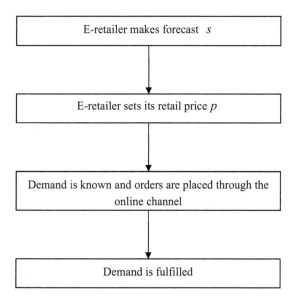

Figure 1.3: Market information and online retailer's expected profit

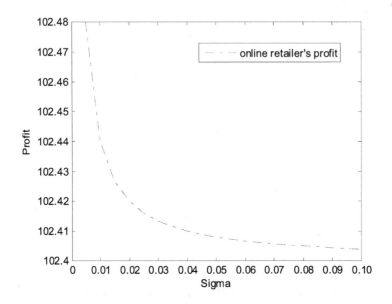

Figure 1.4: The effect of a change in market information on the online retailer's expected profit when the product web-fit is larger

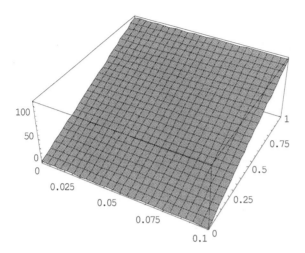

The X axis (0-0.1) of Figure 3 stands for market information, σ;

The Z axis (0-1) of Figure 3 stands for product web-fit, θ;

The Y axis (0-100) of Figure 3 stands for online retailer's expected profit, $E[\pi]$.

Figure 1.5: The effect of a change in market information on the online retailer's

expected profit when product quality is higher

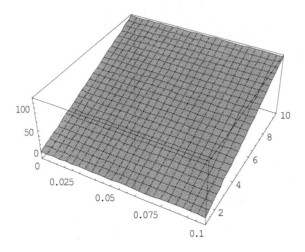

The X axis (0-0.1) of Figure 3 stands for market information, σ;

The Z axis (1-10) of Figure 3 stands for product quality, θ;

The Y axis (0-100) of Figure 3 stands for online retailer's expected profit, $E[\pi]$.

Appendix 1:

Because

$$E(\pi \mid s) = p[E(R - \frac{p}{\theta q}) \mid s)]$$
(A1)

Where p is the abbreviated form of $p(s)$,

And

$$E(R \mid s) = (1-t)\overline{R} + ts$$
(A2)

Substituting (A2) into (A1), and then differentiating of the expected profit, $E(\pi \mid s)$, on p, so we obtain the optimal pricing setting and advertising spending as follows,

$$p = \frac{q\theta\overline{R}}{2} + \frac{q\theta}{2}t(s - \overline{R})$$
(A3)

Then substituting (A3) into (A1), we obtain:

$$E[\pi \mid s] = \frac{q\theta(\overline{R} + (s - \overline{R})t)^2}{4}$$
(A4)

Because $E[(s - \overline{R})^2] = \tau_q + \sigma$ and $t = \frac{\tau_q}{\sigma + \tau_q}$,

After some computation, then we obtain:

$$E[\pi] = \frac{1}{4}q\theta\overline{R}^2 + \frac{q\theta\tau_q^2}{4(\sigma + \tau_q)}$$
(A5)

Therefore, by differentiating of $E[\pi]$ on τ_q, we obtain:

$$\frac{\partial E(\pi)}{\partial \tau_q} = \frac{q\tau_q \theta(2\sigma + \tau_q)}{4(\sigma + \tau_q)^2} > 0$$

Furthermore, by differentiating of $\frac{\partial E[\pi]}{\partial \tau_q}$ on θ, we obtain:

$$\frac{\partial(\frac{\partial E(\pi)}{\partial \tau_q})}{\partial \theta} = \frac{q\tau_q(2\sigma + \tau_q)}{4(\sigma + \tau_q)^2} > 0$$

Thus, proposition 1 is proved.

Appendix 2

Because $E[\pi] = \frac{1}{4}q\theta\bar{R}^2 + \frac{q\theta\tau_q^2}{4(\sigma + \tau_q)}$,

By differentiating of $E(\pi)$ on σ, we obtain:

$$\frac{\partial E(\pi)}{\partial \sigma} = -\frac{q\tau_q^2\theta}{4(\sigma + \tau_q)^2} < 0$$

Furthermore, by differentiating $\frac{\partial E[\pi]}{\partial \sigma}$ with respect to θ, we obtain:

$$\frac{\partial(\frac{\partial E[\pi]}{\partial \sigma})}{\partial \theta} = -\frac{q\tau_q^2}{4(\sigma + \tau_q)^2} < 0$$

Thus, proposition 2 is proved.

Appendix 3

Because $E[\pi] = \frac{1}{4}q\theta\overline{R}^2 + \frac{q\theta\tau_q^2}{4(\sigma + \tau_q)}$,

By differentiating of $E(\pi)$ on σ, we obtain:

$$\frac{\partial E(\pi)}{\partial \sigma} = -\frac{q\tau_q^2\theta}{4(\sigma + \tau_q)^2} < 0$$

Furthermore, by differentiating $\dfrac{\partial E[\pi]}{\partial \sigma}$ with respect to q, we obtain:

$$\frac{\partial(\frac{\partial E[\pi]}{\partial \sigma})}{\partial q} = -\frac{\theta\tau_q^2}{4(\sigma + \tau_q)^2} < 0$$

Thus, proposition 3 is proved.

Appendix 4

Because $E[\pi] = \frac{1}{4}q\theta\overline{R}^2 + \frac{q\theta\tau_q^2}{4(\sigma + \tau_q)}$,

By differentiating of $E(\pi)$ on σ, we obtain:

$$\frac{\partial E(\pi)}{\partial \sigma} = -\frac{q\tau_q^2\theta}{4(\sigma + \tau_q)^2} < 0$$

Furthermore, by differentiating $\dfrac{\partial E[\pi]}{\partial \sigma}$ with respect to $\overline{R}$, we obtain:

$$\frac{\partial(\frac{\partial E[\pi]}{\partial \sigma})}{\partial \overline{R}} = 0$$

Thus, proposition 4 is proved.

CHAPTER TWO

MARKET INFORMATON AND DUAL-CHANNEL PRICING STRATEGIES

IN A MULTI-CHANNEL RETAILER

2.1. Introduction

There are a number of statistical reports from the industry and the government that show that commerce on the Internet is growing at an attractive rate. For instance, according to eMarketer.com, total e-commerce sales are estimated at $108.7 billion in 2006, an increase of 23.5% from 2005. Total retail sales in 2006 increased 5.8% from 2005. E-commerce sales accounted for 2.8% of total sales in 2006, and 2.4% of total sales in 2005. Again according to the Department of Commerce, quarterly e-commerce sales in the fourth quarter of 2006 increased 20.4% from the fourth quarter of 2005. As a consequence, the rapid development of commerce on the Internet has made it attractive for many retailers to engage in direct online sales. There are many reasons for this. First, the expanding role of the Internet in consumer and business procurement activity has created unprecedented opportunities for easy and vast access to customers and for firms. Secondly, the economics of materials delivery have been revolutionized by third-party shipping such as Federal Express and UPS. As a result, many retailers are using or pursuing both online and distributor-based approaches in parallel to sell products. Multi-channel retailing nowadays is becoming more prevalent through the business world.

Since an online channel does compete directly with the traditional retail channel, an important question is how the optimal pricing strategy should be employed by the online and traditional channel stores when the multi-channel retailer uses a mixed online and traditional channel to sell its products, so that each channel store can optimizing its profit, especially, when the market demand is uncertain and information is becoming a critical resource. In our research we focus on the pressing question of dual-channel pricing strategy of a multi-channel retailer under different market structures with demand certainty and uncertainty. We use a game theoretical model to specifically study the following questions: Under the demand certainty, what is the mix pricing strategy that online and traditional channel stores should adopt for the online and traditional retail channels? Under the demand uncertainty, what are the optimal pricing strategy and information value?

The rest of our paper is organized as follows. Section 2 provides a summary of the relevant literature. Section 3 presents our modeling framework. Section 4 studies the pricing strategy under two different types of market structures with demand certainty: the Bertrand game and channel integrated cases. Section 5 studies the pricing strategy under two different types of market structures with demand uncertainty. Concluding remarks are presented in section 6.

2.2. Literature Review

In this section, we review the relevant marketing literature to position our paper. First, we review some of the papers that examine issues that arise when firms sell product through multiple channels under demand certainty. In particular, we focus on those papers that explicitly account for the presence of the Internet channel. Next, we review some of the papers that related to multiple channels with demand uncertainty.

2.2.1. Multi-channel market with demand certainty

There is a long marketing tradition of studying issues that arise from selling across multiple channels. With the emergence of the Internet as a viable channel of distribution, study of multi-channel competition has acquired an additional importance. Researchers have examined a variety of issues. Balasubramanian (1998) modeled competition between the direct and traditional retail channels from a strategic perspective. The level of information disseminated by the direct marketer is shown to have strategic implications, and the author showed that level of market coverage can be used as a mechanism to control competition. Rhee and Park (1999) studied the multiple channel design problem when there are two distinct consumer segments: a price-sensitive segment and a service-sensitive segment. They showed that multiple channels are optimal when the segments are similar in the values that they assign to the retail services. Levary and Mathieu (2000) studied the profits of physical retail stores, online stores, and hybrid retails. They argued that, in the future, hybrid retails would have the maximum optimal profits. Geyskens, Gielens and Dekimpe (2002) found that powerful firms with a few direct channels achieve better financial performance than less powerful firms with broader direct market offerings. King, Sen and Xia (2004) used a game-theoretic approach to study the impact of Web-based e-commerce on a retailer's distribution channel strategy. They showed that the multi-channel strategy followed by retail firms is an equilibrium outcome of the game resulting from competitive pressure by other retailers and this strategy is not the only possible short-run outcome.

Some of the studies specifically focus on the price competition between online retailers and brick and mortar retailers. For instance, Brynjolfsson and Smith (2000) showed through an empirical study that the prices are 9-16% lower on the Internet than in conventional outlets. Smith et al. (2000) did empirical study to show that online prices for digital products are lower than traditional brick and mortar prices. Cattani, Gilland, Heese and Swaminathan (2006), Chiang, Chhajed, and Hess (2003) use a game theoretic model to study the price competition between a manufacturer's direct channel and its traditional channel partner. They argue that the vertically integrated direct channel allows a manufacturer to constrain the partner retailer's pricing behavior and this may not always be detrimental to the retailer because it may be accompanied by wholesale price reduction. However, all of these papers did not consider the situation of demand uncertainty, which limited their application to real business.

2.2.2. Multi-channel market with demand uncertainty

Demand uncertainty has made information so valuable for managers to plan in a multiple-channel market. The importance of information has led to research on a number of different areas. Vives (1984) examined the value of private information to the firms in Cournot and Bertrand competitions and found that the private information always is valuable to the firms. Morrison and Schmittlein (1991) did the research on the best way of combining forecasts obtained from different sources. Blattberg and Hoch (1990) examined how managers combine information they obtain from models with their own personal judgments. Padmanabhan and Rao (1993) have examined situations that how one designs warranty provisions when the quality of the product is uncertain and affected by consumer actions. Day (1990) examined the advantages of using market information versus competitive information in developing firm strategy and Glazer (1991) examined how industry characteristics affect information use and value. Both of papers have proposed conceptual frameworks to understand the impact of superior information on firm performance. Sarvary and Parker (1997) studied the value of marketing information by a competitive analysis and showed that the nature of competition changes qualitatively with a continuous change in basic product-attribute levels. Raju and Roy (2000) examined the impact of market information on the firm performance. Their results showed that information always is more valuable in more competitive industries and for larger firms. However, all of these papers just focused on the traditional channels, not involved in the online verse traditional retail channels.

Our paper addresses these limitations and fills a conceptual and practical gap for a structured analysis of the current state of knowledge about the pricing strategy of online and traditional retail channels. In this paper, we will examine the pricing strategy between online and traditional retail channels under two types of market structures with demand certainty and uncertainty: the Bertrand competition and vertically integrated cases. Under the Bertrand model, the online and traditional channel stores choose their prices on the respective online and traditional retail channels without knowing the other channels store's pricing decision. Under the channel integrated system, the firm determines all optimal pricing strategy for the online and traditional retail channels to maximize the integrated system profit.

2.3. Model Framework

In this section, we lay out our basic market structure.

2.3.1. The online and traditional channel demand functions

We consider a market setting where online channel and traditional brick and mortar channel sell the same product, and compete with each other.

Take in Figure 2.1

In this market, customers can purchase the product from either the online channel or the traditional channel. Assume that consumers are heterogeneous in the valuation of the product. We denote the consumption product value by v. If the price of the product in a traditional channel is p_2, then the consumer surplus in the traditional channel would be $v - p_2$. All consumers with positive consumer surplus (i.e., v is greater than p_2) will buy this product at the traditional channel. The marginal consumer whose valuation v^r equals p_2 is indifferent between buying from the traditional channel or not at all.

The value obtained by consumers when the same product is purchased online would be less than v. We capture the decrease in value by the parameter θ, which stands for web-product fit and is $0 < \theta < 1$. Products that are most likely to sell on the web have web-product compatibility close to one and those that are less likely to sell have web-product fit close to zero. Therefore, the value of the product when purchased on the web is θv. If the price of the product at an online store is p_1 , the

resulting consumer surplus would be $\theta v - p_1$. All consumers whose consumer surplus

at the online is positive (i.e., $\theta v - p_1 \geq 0$) would consider buying from the online store.

The marginal consumer whose value v^d equals p_1/θ is indifferent to buying from

the online channel, or not at all.

Since consumers can buy from either channel, they would prefer the channel where

they derive more surplus (i.e., the online or the traditional retailer:

$\theta v - p_1$ versus $v - p_2$). If $v - p_2 \geq \theta v - p_1$, then the traditional channel would be

weakly preferred to the online channel. The marginal consumer would be one who is

indifferent between the two channels and whose value v^{dr} equals $(p_2 - p_1)/1-\theta$.

Consumers, whose value exceeds this, would prefer the traditional channel. It can be

shown that when $v^d < v^r$, then $v^d < v^r < v^{dr}$, and when $v^d > v^r$, then $v^d > v^r > v^{dr}$.

In the former, all consumers with valuation in the interval $[v^d, v^{dr}]$ prefer to buy from

the online, and all those in the interval $[v^{dr}, v]$ prefer to buy from the traditional

channel. Those consumers whose valuations are in $[0, v^d]$ decline to buy the product

from either of two channels. In the latter case, no customers want to buy from the

online, and all those consumers whose valuations are in the interval $[v^r, v]$ buy from

the traditional channel. Chiang, Chhajed and Hess (2003) have used a similar market

structure. Thus, the demands for the online and traditional channels, respectively, can

be expressed as

$$d_1 = \begin{cases} \dfrac{\theta p_2 - p_1}{\theta(1-\theta)} & p_2 \geq \dfrac{p_1}{\theta} \\ 0 & otherwise \end{cases} \qquad (1)$$

$$d_2 = \begin{cases} v - \dfrac{p_2 - p_1}{1 - \theta} & p_2 \geq \dfrac{p_1}{\theta} \\ v - p_2 & otherwise \end{cases} \qquad (2)$$

Where, d_1 is the demand at the online channel and d_2 is the demand at the traditional channel.

2.3.2. Profit functions of online and traditional channel stores

Here we assume that the marginal costs for online and traditional channel stores are c_1 and c_2, respectively. However, in order to simplify exposition, we assume $c_1 = c_2 = 0$ without affecting the basic results. Consequently, in a given period, the online channel store's profit would be,

$$\pi_1 = p_1 d_1 \qquad (3)$$

Similarly, a traditional channel store's profit would be,

$$\pi_2 = p_2 d_2 \qquad (4)$$

The total profit of the two channel stores can then be written as,

$$\pi_I = p_1 d_1 + p_2 d_2 \qquad (5)$$

If the multi-channel retailer integrates the two channels, unified and centralized price solutions are sought to maximize the total profit of the integrated system. Otherwise if these two channels are not integrated, competitive prices are then sought for two individual channels. For the competitive pricing case, we consider in this paper the essence of most of the competitions between the online and traditional channel stores: the Bertrand competition. In what follows, we first consider optimal pricing strategy under the Bertrand competition setting. We then analyze the equilibrium prices for the integrated system.

2.4. The Certainty Model

2.4.1. Non-integrated competitive pricing strategy

For the case where the two channels (online and traditional channels) are not integrated, competitive pricing strategies are then sought while each channel store strives to maximize individual profit with consideration of interaction with opponent. In what follows, we study the competitive pricing strategy under the Bertrand competition equilibrium.

2.4.2. Price strategy under Bertrand competition with demand certainty

In this section, we will discuss the pricing strategy under the Bertrand competition equilibrium. In Bertrand competition, the online and traditional channel stores have an equal power in the market. The online store sells product by online channel and determine its price p_1, so online store can maximize its profit π_1. The traditional channel store declares a retail price p_2 independently uninformed price p_1, so as to maximize its profit π_2.

Let p_1^B, p_2^B denote the online and traditional retail prices under the Bertrand competition equilibrium, respectively. Now, the two retailers play a Bertrand game of profit maximization to decide simultaneously the online and traditional retail prices (p_1^B, p_2^B). The relationship between the online and traditional channel stores is symmetrical in this competition. There is no price leader in this market, and both channel stores make price decisions independently of each other.

Given the above structure, we obtain the Bertrand pricing strategy.

Proposition 1: *Suppose the online and traditional channel stores play a Bertrand game to maximize their respective profits, π_1 and π_2. Then, there exists optimal Bertrand competitive pricing strategy (p_1^B, p_2^B), which can be determined as follows:*

$$p_1^B = \frac{v\theta(1-\theta)}{4-\theta}$$

$$p_2^B = \frac{2v(1-\theta)}{4-\theta}$$

Proof: Please see Appendix 1 for proof.

Proposition 1 shows that in a competitive market, the optimal pricing strategy for online and traditional channel stores to adopt are (p_1^B, p_2^B). In other word, the online price should be lower than the traditional retail price. Our results in proposition 2 are consistent with the findings in Wigand and Benjamin (1995), Bakos (1997), Brynjolfsson and Smith (2000), Johannes (2000), Chiang, Chhajed and Hess (2003), etc. They all show that adopting such a pricing strategy can effectively maximize channel store's individual profit.

2.4.3. Pricing strategy under vertically integrated system with demand certainty

However, if the two channels are integrated, the decision-making in an integrated system is centralized at the multi-channel retailer. Therefore, with centralized decision making, the multi-channel retailer's integrated problem of pricing the mixed distribution channel can be stared as: determine a pricing strategy (p_1^I, p_2^I) for both online and traditional retail channels, so that the total profit of the whole integrated system is maximized, which can be expressed as the following maximization problem:

$$Max\pi_I = \pi_1 + \pi_2 = p_1 d_1 + p_2 d_2 \qquad (6)$$

Maximizing this equation with respect to p_1^I and p_2^I, we have proposition 2.

Proposition 2: *For an integrated online and traditional retail system, let p_1^I and p_2^I denote the pricing decisions for online and traditional retail channels. Then, the optimal centralized pricing strategy (p_1^I, p_2^I) can be determined as follows:*

$$p_1^I = \frac{v\theta}{2}$$

$$p_2^I = \frac{v}{2}$$

Proof: Please see Appendix 2 for proof.

The prices (p_1^I, p_2^I) maximize the overall profit $\pi_I = \pi_1 + \pi_2$. However, one of the channel stores might not be sequentially optimized in the integrated system in the sense that each channel store makes its own decisions with no regard to the impact on the other channel store in the non-integrated system. Therefore, a coordination mechanism is needed to coordinate the online and traditional stores to achieve overall optimization. Typically, profit sharing policy may be used to as incentive to coordinate the system and ensure the success of channel integration. Proposition 1 shows that the online price should be lower than the traditional retail price. It turns out that this result holds for the integrated case as well in proposition 2.

2.5. The Uncertainty Model

In this section, we consider the model advanced in the last section but now with a demand uncertainty.

Insert in Figure 2.2 here

$$t_i = \frac{V}{\sigma_i + V}, \quad i = 1,2. \tag{9}$$

t_i is referred to as the precision parameter and it is inversely proportional to the error variance σ_i. As σ_i ranges from ∞ to 0, the forecast goes from being perfectly informative to being not informative at all and at the same time t_i ranges from 1 to 0. When the information is perfect, $E(v \mid f_i) = f_i$, $i = 1,2,$ when there is no information, $E(v \mid f_i) = \bar{v}$, $i = 1,2.$

Because V is the variance of the random demand intercept, thus the conditional expectation of one channel's forecast given the other channel' forecast can be expressed as follows:

$$E(f_j \mid f_i) = (1 - d_i)\bar{v} + d_i f_i, \quad i = 1,2; \quad j = 3 - i, \tag{10}$$

Where

$$d_i = \frac{V + \sigma}{V + \sigma_i}, \quad i = 1,2. \text{(Cyert and DeGroot 1970, 1973; Vives 1984)} \tag{11}$$

The proposed information model structure also suggests that

$$E[(f_i - \bar{v})^2] = E[(e + \varepsilon_i)^2] = V + \sigma_i, \quad i = 1,2 \tag{12}$$

When the online and traditional channel stores are in an integrated system, the integrated firm has the full forecast information of both the online and traditional channels. Thus, the expected estimate about v is $f_I = E(v \mid f_1, f_2)$, which is based on the new information gathered together from the two channel stores. Thus,

$$E(v \mid f_I) = (1 - t_I)\bar{v} + t_I f_I, \quad \text{where } t_I = \frac{\sigma_I}{\sigma_I + V}$$

2.5.1. Pricing strategy under Bertrand competition with demand uncertainty

The online and traditional channel stores choose their respective prices to maximize their own expected profit-in this manner the two channels compete. The retail price of the other channel is taken as given. In other words, we assume that competition between channels is of the independent, Bertrand type. Thus, the expected profit for online and traditional channel stores can be expressed as follows:

$$E(\pi_1^B \mid f_1) = p_1[E(\frac{p_2 - p_1}{1-\theta} - \frac{p_1}{\theta} \mid f_1)] \tag{13}$$

$$E(\pi_2^B \mid f_2) = p_2[E(v - \frac{p_2 - p_1}{1-\theta} \mid f_2)] \tag{14}$$

Where p_1 and p_2 are the abbreviated forms of $p_1(f_1)$ and $p_2(f_1)$, respectively; $E[\pi_1^B]$ is the expected profit of online channel store and $E[\pi_2^B]$ is the expected profit of traditional channel store. Given the above structure, we can find the Bertrand pricing strategy under uncertain market demand.

Proposition 3: *In the Bertrand competition with uncertain demand, the optimal pricing strategy for the online and traditional channel stores can be determined as follows:*

$$p_1^B(f_1) = \frac{\bar{v}\theta(1-\theta)}{4-\theta} + \frac{d_2\theta(1-\theta)}{4-d_1d_2\theta}t_1(f_1 - \bar{v})$$

$$p_2^B(f_2) = \frac{2\bar{v}(1-\theta)}{4-\theta} + \frac{2(1-\theta)}{4-d_1d_2\theta}t_2(f_2 - \bar{v})$$

Proof: Please see Appendix 3 for proof.

The above Bertrand price functions show that if market demand is uncertain, each channel store obtains a forecast about v, and includes this into its pricing strategy. For online channel store, the optimal pricing in proposition 3 is a function of the difference between the forecast f_1 and $\bar{v}$. This difference is weighted by the

term $\dfrac{d_2\theta(1-\theta)}{4-d_1d_2\theta}t_1$, since t_1 reflects the accuracy of online channel forecast. If the

forecasts are completely uninformative($\sigma_1 = \sigma_2 = \infty$, which is $t_1 = t_2 \approx 0$), then each

channel store will not use its forecast and use only the prior mean $\bar{v}$. The optimal

prices will be $p_1^B(f_1) = \dfrac{\bar{v}\theta(1-\theta)}{4-\theta}$ and $p_2^B(f_2) = \dfrac{2\bar{v}(1-\theta)}{4-\theta}$. If both forecasts are

perfectly accurate ($\sigma_1 = \sigma_2 = 0$, which is $t_1 = t_2 \approx 1$ and $d_1 = d_2 \approx 1$), then each

channel store will use only its forecast for its price, which is not depend on the prior

mean $\bar{v}$. The optimal prices will be $p_1^B(f_1) = \dfrac{f_1\theta(1-\theta)}{4-\theta}$ and

$p_2^B(f_2) = \dfrac{2f_2\theta(1-\theta)}{4-\theta}$. However, in general, the forecast is not perfect, the optimal

pricing strategy will be a combination of prior mean $\bar{v}$ and forecast f_i, $i = 1,2$.

Just as we know, the bottom line is the profit and not the prices. Therefore, it

is critical to find out the affect of information accuracy on the profits of online and

traditional channel stores. Thus, the online and traditional channel stores can adopt

optimal strategy to derive more profits. This can be determined by examining the

effect of information accuracy on the profits of online and traditional channel stores in

the Bertrand competition equilibrium. The results show that in Bertrand competition,

the expected profits of both the online and traditional channel stores increase with the

accuracy of their respective forecast information. Furthermore, by comparing the

effect of information accuracy on the profit of online and traditional channel stores,

we obtain proposition 4,

Proposition 4: *In Bertrand competition, the effect of a change in traditional channel store's information accuracy on the expected profit of traditional channel store is larger than the effect of a change in online store's information accuracy on the expected profit of online store.*

Proof: Please see Appendix 4 for proof.

Proposition 4 shows that in a competitive market, information accuracy plays a more important role in the traditional channel store's profit than in the online store's profit. That means that information accuracy is more valuable to the traditional channel store.

This is to be expected because online retail sales have been a small portion of overall retail sales. From US Census Bureau, online retail sales only accounted for 2.8 percent of all retail sales in 2006 and 2.4 percent of total retail sales in 2005.

We now continue to examine whether an increase in information accuracy provides better competitive advantage to traditional channel store than to online store, and vice verse. The main results are summarized as follows.

Proposition 5: *In Bertrand competition, the difference between the expected profit in the online store and the expected profit in the traditional channel store, $E[\pi_2^B] - E[\pi_1^B]$, always increases with either channel's information accuracy.*

Proof: Please see Appendix 5 for proof.

Proposition 5 shows that the traditional channel store always profits more from the improvement in information accuracy than the online channel store. This is to be expected because the traditional retail sales have been dominating the market of overall retail sales, thus it benefits more when the information accuracy is improved.

2.5.2. Pricing strategy under integrated system with demand uncertainty

In the integrated system, the multi-channel retailer selects the pricing strategy of online and traditional retail channels to maximize its total profit under the Bayesian forecast. Thus, the expected profit for the integrated firm can be expressed as follows:

$$E(\pi_I \mid f_I) = E(\pi_1 \mid f_I) + E(\pi_2 \mid f_I) = p_1[E(\frac{p_2 - p_1}{1-\theta} - \frac{p_1}{\theta} \mid f_I)] + p_2[E(v - \frac{p_2 - p_1}{1-\theta} \mid f_I)]$$

Where p_1 and p_2 are the abbreviated forms of $p_1(f_I)$ and $p_2(f_I)$, respectively; π_I is the total profit of the online and traditional retail channel stores in an integrated system.

Next, we solve for the specific affine functions that constitute the equilibrium prices. Thus, the optimal pricing strategies of integrated system are determined as follows.

Proposition 6: *The unique Bayesian pricing strategy in the integrated firm is* $(p_1^I(f_I), p_2^I(f_I))$, *which can be determined as*

$$p_1^I(f_I) = \frac{\overline{v}\theta}{2} + \frac{\theta}{2}t_I(f_I - \overline{v})$$

$$p_2^I(f_I) = \frac{1}{2}\overline{v} + \frac{1}{2}t_I(f_I - \overline{v})$$

Proof: Please see Appendix 6 for proof.

Proposition 6 shows that in an integrated system, if the forecasts are completely uninformative ($\sigma_I = \infty$, which is $t_I \approx 0$), the optimal prices will be $p_1^I(f_I) = \frac{\overline{v}\theta}{2}$ and $p_2^I(f_I) = \frac{\overline{v}}{2}$. If both forecasts are perfectly accurate ($\sigma_I = 0$, which is $t_I \approx 1$), the optimal prices will be $p_1^I(f_I) = \frac{f_I\theta}{2}$ and $p_2^I(f_2) = \frac{f_I}{2}$. The optimal pricing strategies ($p_1(f_I)$, $p_2(f_I)$) effectively maximizes the expected profit of whole integrated system.

We also examine the affect of information accuracy on the expected profit of whole integrated system and find out that in the integrated system, the expected profit increases with information accuracy as well. These results show that more accurate information always contributes to improving integrated firm's overall profit. We then continue to examine the effect of information accuracy on the channel stores' profits in the integrated case. Then, we obtain our proposition 7.

Proposition 7: *In the integrated system, the expected profit of the traditional channel store increases with its information accuracy, but the expected profit of the online store is unaffected by its information accuracy.*

Proof: Please see Appendix 7 for proof.

The result in proposition 7 is consistent with the finding in Chiang, et al (2003) that it is most profitable for an integrated firm to arrange prices so that nothing is ever sold through its own online channel. Thus, information accuracy only has an impact on the traditional retail channel. In other words, information is more valuable to traditional channel store in the integrated case, too.

2.6. Concluding Remarks

In this paper, we demonstrate that optimal pricing strategies exist under either the integrated or Bertrand competition models with demand certainty and uncertainty in a mixed online and traditional retail distribution channels, and we further obtain equilibrium prices for both the integrated system and Bertrand game. Our results indicate that when the market demand is certain, the optimal pricing strategy for online and traditional channel store to adopt is to use a low-high pricing strategy. In other words, typically, the online price should be lower than the traditional retail price, no matter the online and traditional channels are in the integrated system or Bertrand competition case. However, if the market demand is uncertain, the information accuracy strategically impacts on the setting of pricing strategy for online and traditional channels and further impacts on the overall profits of channel stores. Information accuracy always is more valuable to the traditional channel store, no matter it is in a competitive or integrated market. These results from our research provide important insights for business market managers.

This research can be extended in several directions in future work. First, in this paper our analysis is based on a single period model, therefore, for future potential research, it is a good idea to examine the mix pricing strategies in a dynamic multi-period environment. Second, information is assumed to be costless in this research, thus this research can also be extended to include other variables, such as information cost, in order to continue studying the influence and impacts of external factors relative to the information accuracy. In the future, aside from considering other factors, we can extend our study to include more retailers in a competitive market. Since the value of information accuracy has been of interest to researchers and practitioners, further research can be carried out on the methods and plans used by information pooling and sharing between channel members.

Figure 2.1: Mixed online and traditional retail distribution system

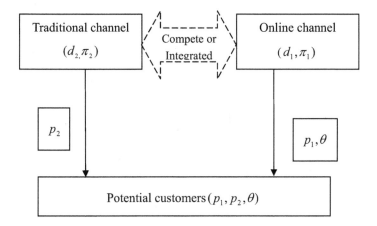

The followings are the definitions of the symbols that appear in Figure 2.1.

π_1 : Online channel store's profit

π_2 : Traditional channel store's profit

d_1 : Demand in the online channel

d_2 : Demand in the traditional channel

p_1 : Price in the online channel

p_2 : Price in the traditional retail channel

θ : Denotes the web-product fit

Figure 2.2: The information forecast diagram

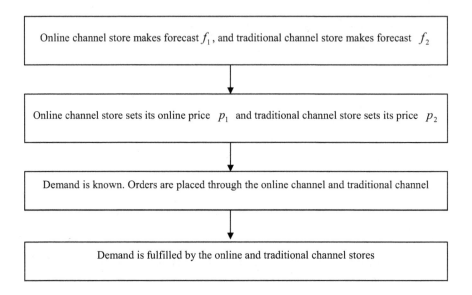

Additional symbols are used in Figure 2.2 are:

f_1 : Online channel store's forecast

f_2 : Traditional channel store's forecast

Appendix 1

$$d_1 = \begin{cases} \dfrac{\theta p_2 - p_1}{\theta(1-\theta)} & p_2 \geq \dfrac{p_1}{\theta} \\ 0 & otherwise \end{cases}$$
(A1)

$$d_2 = \begin{cases} v - \dfrac{p_2 - p_1}{1-\theta} & p_2 \geq \dfrac{p_1}{\theta} \\ v - p_2 & otherwise \end{cases}, $$
(A2)

The profit for the online channel store is as follows:

$$\pi_1 = p_1 d_1$$
(A3)

Similarly for the traditional channel store, the profit is as follows:

(A4)
$$\pi_2 = p_2 d_2$$

Under Bertrand competition, we differentiate π_1 on p_1 and π_2 on p_2 and let $(\partial \pi_1 / \partial p_1) = 0$ and $(\partial \pi_2 / \partial p_2) = 0$. Then, by substituting p_1 into p_2, we obtain:

$$p_2^B = \frac{2v(1-\theta)}{4-\theta}$$
(A5)

Similarly, we obtain:

$$p_1^B = \frac{v\theta(1-\theta)}{4-\theta}$$
(A6)

Thus, proposition 1 is proved.

Appendix 2

Because the total profit of an integrated firm is:

$$\pi_I = p_1 d_1 + p_2 d_2$$
(A7)

By differentiating π_I on p_1 and p_2 simultaneously and letting $(\partial \pi_I / \partial p_1) = 0$ and $(\partial \pi_I / \partial p_2) = 0$, we obtain:

$$p_1^I = \frac{v\theta}{2}$$
(A8)

$$p_2^I = \frac{v}{2} \qquad\qquad\qquad\qquad (A9)$$

Thus, proposition 2 is proved.

Appendix 3

Because

$$E(\pi_1^B \mid f_1) = p_1[E(\frac{p_2 - p_1}{1-\theta} - \frac{p_1}{\theta} \mid f_1)] \qquad\qquad (A10)$$

$$E(\pi_2^B \mid f_2) = p_2[E(v - \frac{p_2 - p_1}{1-\theta} \mid f_2)] \qquad\qquad (A11)$$

And

$$E(v \mid f_i) = (1 - t_i)\overline{v} + t_i f_i, \quad i = 1,2; \; j = 3 - i, \qquad\qquad (A12)$$

$$E(f_j \mid f_i) = (1 - d_i)\overline{v} + d_i f_i, \quad i = 1,2; \; j = 3 - i, \qquad\qquad (A13)$$

$$E[(f_i - \overline{v})^2] = E[(e + \varepsilon_i)^2] = V + \sigma_i, \quad i = 1,2 \qquad\qquad (A14)$$

Substituting (A12) into (A10) and (A11), and we differentiate the expected profits, $E(\pi_1^B \mid f_1)$, on p_1 and $E(\pi_2^B \mid f_2)$ on p_2 simultaneously. We then solve the equations, and after some computation, we obtain the optimal pricing strategies under the Bertrand competition game as follows,

$$p_1^B(f_1) = \frac{\overline{v}\theta(1-\theta)}{4-\theta} + \frac{d_2\theta(1-\theta)}{4 - d_1 d_2 \theta} t_1(f_1 - \overline{v}) \qquad\qquad (A15)$$

$$p_2^B(f_2) = \frac{2\overline{v}(1-\theta)}{4-\theta} + \frac{2(1-\theta)}{4 - d_1 d_2 \theta} t_2(f_2 - \overline{v}) \qquad\qquad (A16)$$

Thus, proposition 3 is proved.

Appendix 4

Substituting (A15) and (A16) into (A10) and (A11), we obtain:

$$E[\pi_1^B] = \frac{\overline{v}^2 \theta(1-\theta)}{(4-\theta)^2} + \frac{d_2^2 \theta N t_1 (1-\theta)}{(4-d_1 d_2 \theta)^2} \tag{A17}$$

$$E[\pi_2^B] = \frac{4\overline{v}^2(1-\theta)}{(4-\theta)^2} + \frac{4V t_2(1-\theta)}{(4-d_1 d_2 \theta)^2} \tag{A18}$$

Where

$$t_i = \frac{V}{\sigma_i + V}, \tag{A19}$$

And

$$d_i = \frac{V+\sigma}{V+\sigma_i}, \quad i = 1,2. \tag{A20}$$

Substituting (A19) and (A20) into (A17) and (A18), and then differentiating with respect to σ_1 and σ_2, respectively, we obtain

$$\frac{\partial E[\pi_1^B]}{\partial \sigma_1} = -\frac{V^2\theta(1-\theta)(V+\sigma)^2(4\sigma_1\sigma_2 + V^2(4+\theta) + \sigma^2\theta + 2V(2\sigma_1 + 2\sigma_2 + \sigma\theta))}{(4\sigma_1\sigma_2 + V^2(4-\theta) - \sigma^2\theta + V(4\sigma_1 + 4\sigma_2 - 2\sigma\theta))^3} < 0 \tag{A21}$$

$$\frac{\partial E[\pi_2^B]}{\partial \sigma_2} = -\frac{4V^2\theta(1-\theta)(V+\sigma_1)^2(4\sigma_1\sigma_2 + V^2(4+\theta) + \sigma^2\theta + 2V(2\sigma_1 + 2\sigma_2 + \sigma\theta))}{(4\sigma_1\sigma_2 + V^2(4-\theta) - \sigma^2\theta + V(4\sigma_1 + 4\sigma_2 - 2\sigma\theta))^3} < 0 \tag{A22}$$

So let (A21) subtract (A22), we obtain

$$\frac{\partial E[\pi_1^B]}{\partial \sigma_1} - \frac{\partial E[\pi_2^B]}{\partial \sigma_2} = \frac{V^2\theta(1-\theta)(4(V+\sigma_1)^2 + (V+\sigma)^2\theta)(4\sigma_1\sigma_2 + V^2(4+\theta) + \sigma^2\theta + 2V(2\sigma_1 + 2\sigma_2 + \sigma\theta))}{(4\sigma_1\sigma_2 + V^2(4-\theta) - \sigma^2\theta + V(4\sigma_1 + 4\sigma_2 - 2\sigma\theta))^3} > 0$$

$$\tag{A23}$$

Thus, proposition 4 is proved.

Appendix 5

Because

$$E[\pi_1^B] = \frac{\bar{v}^2\theta(1-\theta)}{(4-\theta)^2} + \frac{d_2^2\theta V t_1(1-\theta)}{(4-d_1d_2\theta)^2}$$ (A24)

$$E[\pi_2^B] = \frac{4\bar{v}^2(1-\theta)}{(4-\theta)^2} + \frac{4V t_2(1-\theta)}{(4-d_1d_2\theta)^2}$$ (A25)

Where

$$t_i = \frac{V}{\sigma_i + V},$$ (A26)

And

$$d_i = \frac{V+\sigma}{V+\sigma_i}, \quad i=1,2.$$ (A27)

Therefore,

$$\frac{\partial(E[\pi_2^B] - E[\pi_1^B])}{\partial \sigma_1} = -\frac{V^2\theta(1-\theta)(V+\sigma_2)^2}{(4\sigma_1\sigma_2 + V^2(4-\theta) - \sigma^2\theta + V(4\sigma_1 + 4\sigma_2 - 2\sigma\theta))^2} < 0$$

$$\frac{\partial(E[\pi_2^B] - E[\pi_1^B])}{\partial \sigma_2} = -\frac{4V^2\theta(1-\theta)(V+\sigma_1)^2}{(4\sigma_1\sigma_2 + V^2(4-\theta) - \sigma^2\theta + V(4\sigma_1 + 4\sigma_2 - 2\sigma\theta))^2} < 0$$

Thus, proposition 5 is proved.

Appendix 6

Because

$$E(\pi_I \mid f_I) = E(\pi_1^I \mid f_I) + E(\pi_2^I \mid f_I) = p_1[E(\frac{p_2 - p_1}{1-\theta} - \frac{p_1}{\theta} \mid f_I)] + p_2[E(v - \frac{p_2 - p_1}{1-\theta} \mid f_I)]$$ (A28)

And

$$E(v \mid f_I) = (1 - t_I)\bar{v} + t_I f_I, \tag{A29}$$

$$E[(f_I - \bar{v})^2] = E[(e + \varepsilon_I)^2] = V + \sigma_I \tag{A30}$$

$$t_I = \frac{V}{\sigma_I + V}$$

Substituting (A29) into (A28), and we differentiate the expected profits, $E(\pi_I^B \mid f_I)$, on p_1 and p_2 simultaneously. We then solve the equations, and after some computation, we obtain the optimal pricing strategies under the vertically integrated system as follows,

$$p_1^I(f_I) = \frac{\bar{v}\theta}{2} + \frac{\theta}{2} t_I (f_I - \bar{v}) \tag{A31}$$

$$p_2^I(f_I) = \frac{1}{2}\bar{v} + \frac{1}{2} t_I (f_I - \bar{v}) \tag{A32}$$

Thus, proposition 6 is proved.

Appendix 7

Substituting (A31) and (A32) into (A28), we obtain:

$$E[\pi_1^I] = 0 \tag{A33}$$

$$E[\pi_2^I] = \frac{\bar{v}^2}{4} + \frac{V^2}{4(V + \sigma_I)} \tag{A34}$$

Differentiating the expected profits, $E(\pi_1^I)$, on v_I and $E(\pi_2^I)$ on v_I, we obtain

$$\frac{\partial E[\pi_1^I]}{\partial \sigma_I} = 0 \tag{A35}$$

$$\frac{\partial E[\pi_2^I]}{\partial \sigma_I} < 0 \tag{A36}$$

Thus, proposition 7 is proved.

CHAPTER THREE

INFORMATON SHARING IN THE SUPPLY CHAIN OF MANUFACTURER

AND E-RETAILER

3.1. Introduction

The surge in the growth of information systems over the past two decades has significantly reshaped supply chain management and given businesses an unprecedented marketing opportunity. In the US, the business-to-consumer (B2C) sales over the Internet are increasing at an unprecedented rate. The Census Bureau of the Department of Commerce estimated that total e-commerce sales for 2006 were at $108.7 billion, an increase of 23.5 percent from 2005. In the same period, the total retail sales increased by only 5.8%. The growth rate in the e-commerce sales is going to increase even further in the near future. As a result, the growth of the Internet has made it attractive for many retailers or individuals to engage in e-commerce sales, especially for those products that are more suitable for selling through the e-market (Chiang, Chhajed and Hess, 2003).

The significant benefit of information systems is to let firms share information (i.e., demand forecast information, sales trend and data, etc.) quickly and inexpensively. Information sharing can effectively improve the efficiency of supply chain management. The manufacturer and retailer can use the information systems to response to customer demand more quickly and improve the accuracy of demand forecasts by information sharing. There is obviously no doubt that a good information base helps decision making. But can information sharing within a supply chain increase both the manufacturer and retailer profit?

In our research, we focus on the value of demand forecast information sharing in a supply chain consisting of a manufacturer and an e-retailer (e-commerce retailer). We use a game theoretical model to specifically study the following questions: under what condition is information sharing mutually beneficial to both the manufacturer and the e-retailer? Under what condition is only one player better off and the other is worse off with information sharing? Especially, when the market share of e-retailer or the e-market base demand of product category is larger, what is the value of information sharing? Based on our results, we suggest marketing strategies for the supply chain players (the manufacturer and the e-retailer) to adopt. Findings from our research should be of value for the manufacturer and the e-retailer planning on how to improve market information accuracy, which then get transmitted to their profits.

The rest of our paper is organized as follows. Section 2 provides a summary of the relevant literature. Section 3 presents our modeling framework. Section 4 analyzes the cases of no information sharing and information sharing for the manufacturer and the e-retailer. Section 5 studies the value of information sharing for the manufacturer and the e-retailer and how the value of information sharing is further moderated by the market share of the online retailer and the market demand base of product category. We present our simulation results in Section 6. Conclusions and managerial implications are presented in section 7. All relevant proofs are given in the Appendices for clarity of exposition.

3.2. Literature Review

Given the increasing importance of information, researchers have looked at the subject of information from a variety of perspectives. Raju and Roy (2000) provide a good summary of this by discussing the studies done by, among others, Hilton (1981), Vives (1984), Morrison and Schmittlein (1991), Blattberg and Hoch (1990), Padmanabhan and Rao (1993), Day (1990), Glazer (1991), Sarvary and Parker (1997). Raju and Roy (2000) themselves examined the impact of market information on firm performance. Their results showed that information is always more valuable in more competitive industries and for larger firms. Gavirneni, Kapuscinski and Tayur (1999) studied partial and complete shared information of inventory policies between a supplier and a retailer, and they estimated the savings of the supplier due to information sharing and addressed when information sharing was more valuable. Bourland, Powell and Pyke (1996) showed that both the manufacturer and the retailer would profit from information sharing when their ordering cycles were significantly out of phase. Gavirneni, Kapuscinski and Tayur (1999) studied partial and complete shared information of inventory policies between a supplier and a retailer; they estimated the savings of the supplier due to information sharing and indicated when information sharing was more valuable. Cachon and Fisher (2000) investigated the value of information sharing between one supplier and multiple identical retailers.

They found that information sharing led to savings due to lead time and batch size reduction. Lee, So and Tang (2000) looked at the value of information sharing in a two level supply chain and found that information sharing can provide significant inventory reduction and cost savings. Corbett, Zhou and Tang (2004) found that it is better for the supplier to offer a two-part contracts to the buyer once there is full information sharing. Cheng and Wu (2005) researched the impact of information sharing in a two-level supply chain with multiple retailers. They showed that the manufacturer always benefits from the information sharing. Huang, Chu and Lee (2006) examined strategic information sharing in a supply chain. They showed that reducing the cost of sharing information and increasing the profit margin of either the retailer or the vendor will facilitate information sharing. Li and Lin (2006) accessed information sharing and information quality in supply chain management. They showed that trusting in supply chain partners and shared vision between supply chain partners plays a positive influence on the information sharing and information quality, but supplier uncertainty plays a negative influence. Chiang and Feng (2007) found that the manufacturer benefits more from the information sharing than retailers when supply uncertainty and demand volatility are present.

However, so far, all research on information sharing focuses on inventory and logistics and did not consider the important effect of e-retailer's market power and product category on the value of information sharing. Our paper addresses this limitation and fills a conceptual and practical gap for a structured analysis of the current state of knowledge regarding the value of information sharing between the manufacturer and the e-retailer. Our objective of this paper is mainly to show the strategic value of information sharing for the supply chain players when the market power of e-retailer is larger and the product category is more compatible to the e-market.

3.3. Model Framework

In this section, we consider a simple supply chain made up of one manufacturer and one e-retailer.

Insert in Figure 3.1 here

We assume that the manufacturer is the Stackelberg leader and the e-retailer is the follower. We also assume that both the manufacturer and the retailer choose their optimal decision variables to optimize their profits. In the Stackelberg competition model, the manufacturer acting as market leader moves first and sets its wholesale price to optimize its own profit. Subsequently the e-retailer acts as the market follower and sets a price to maximize its profit. The demand is uncertain. Each supply chain player (the manufacturer or the e-retailer) predicts a product's e-market base demand, and this predicted value helps in setting prices.

Specifically, we assume that the e-retailer has some market power and has a downward-sloping demand function given by

$$d = \theta(a - bp) \qquad\qquad (1)$$

3.4.1. No information sharing

In this case, we assume that the manufacturer and the e-retailer maximize their respective expected profits by choosing optimal pricing policies. Thus the expected profit, conditional on their respective forecast, can be expressed as follows:

$$E[\pi_1^N] = E[\theta(w-c)(a-bp) \mid f_1)] \qquad (3)$$

$$E[\pi_2^N] = E[\theta(p-w)(a-bp) \mid f_2)] \qquad (4)$$

Where c the product unit cost, and w is the manufacturer's whole price. π_1^N and π_2^N denote the manufacturer's profit and the e-retailer's profit under no information sharing, respectively. Since the manufacturer is the Stackelberg leader and the retailer is the follower. The equilibrium prices and the corresponding profits are derived in the next proposition.

Proposition 1. *The equilibrium prices for the non-information sharing case are:*

$$w^N = \frac{a_{rs} + bc}{2b} \text{ and } p^N = \frac{2a_s + a_{rs} + bc}{4b}$$

The corresponding profits for each supply chain player are:

$$\pi_1^N = \frac{\theta(2a_s - a_{rs} - bc)(a_{rs} - bc)}{8b} \text{ and } \pi_2^N = \frac{\theta(2a_s - a_{rs} - bc)^2}{16b}$$

Where, w^N and p^N are the wholesale price and e-retail price respectively under no information sharing; and

$$a_s = \overline{Ia} + Jf_1 + Kf_2, \ a_{rs} = \overline{Ia} + Jf_1 + K((1-d_1)\overline{a} + d_1f_1),$$

Where,

$$I = \frac{(1-\rho^2)\sigma_1^2\sigma_2^2}{(1-\rho^2)\sigma_1^2\sigma_2^2 + \sigma_0^2(\sigma_1^2 + \sigma_2^2 - 2\rho\sigma_1\sigma_2)} ,$$

$$J = \frac{\sigma_0^2(\sigma_2^2 - \rho\sigma_1\sigma_2)}{(1-\rho^2)\sigma_1^2\sigma_2^2 + \sigma_0^2(\sigma_1^2 + \sigma_2^2 - 2\rho\sigma_1\sigma_2)} ,$$

$$K = \frac{\sigma_0^2(\sigma_1^2 - \rho\sigma_1\sigma_2)}{(1-\rho^2)\sigma_1^2\sigma_2^2 + \sigma_0^2(\sigma_1^2 + \sigma_2^2 - 2\rho\sigma_1\sigma_2)}$$

Proof: Please see Appendix 1 for proof

From the results in proposition 1, it is shown that the optimal wholesale price for the manufacturer is obtained by using only the manufacturer's forecast. The e-retailer, on the other hand, has knowledge of the manufacturer's forecast before making its price decisions. The results in proposition 1 show that the manufacturer's wholesale price is increasing with f_1 and the e-retailer's retail price is increasing with f_1 and f_2. That means that the more optimistic the manufacturer or the e-retailer feels about the product's e-market base demand, the higher price it will set. Next, we compare these optimal strategies with those using another case in which the manufacturer and the e-retailer share their forecast information with each other.

3.4.2. Information sharing

In this situation, the manufacturer and the e-retailer share the forecasts with each other before marking their respective optimal decisions. Thus the expected profits of supply chain players are:

$$E[\pi_1^S] = E[\theta(w-c)(a-bp) \mid f_1, f_2)] \tag{5}$$

$$E[\pi_2^S] = E[\theta(p-w)(a-bp) \mid f_1, f_2)] \tag{6}$$

Where π_1^S and π_2^S denote the manufacturer profit and the e-retailer profit, respectively, under information sharing with each other. In the next proposition, we derive both the optimal prices and profit of each supply chain player.

Proposition 2. *The equilibrium prices for the information sharing case are:*

$$w^S = \frac{a_S + bc}{2b} \text{ and } p^S = \frac{3a_S + bc}{4b}$$

The corresponding profits for each supply chain player are:

$$\pi_1^S = \frac{\theta(a_S - bc)^2}{8b} \text{ and } \pi_2^S = \frac{\theta(a_S - bc)^2}{16b}$$

Where, w^S and p^S are the wholesale price and e-retail price respectively under information sharing; a_S and a_{rS} are as defined in Proposition 1.

Proof: Please see Appendix 2 for proof

The structure of the price expressions for the information sharing case is similar in form to the price expression in the non-information sharing case. While the former uses both forecasts, f_1 and f_2, the later uses only their own forecasts f_i ($i = 1,2$). The results in proposition 2 also show that under the information sharing setting, if the manufacturer and the e-retailer are more optimistic about the product's e-market base level of demand, they will set higher prices.

3.5. Value of Information Sharing

In order to examine how information sharing affects the profits of the manufacturer and the e-retailer, we compare each player's profit without information sharing in proposition 1 with their profits with information sharing in proposition 2. Then we obtain proposition 3.

Proposition 3: *The manufacturer always benefits from information sharing. However, the e-retailer only benefits from information sharing under the condition of*

$$E[\pi_2^S] > E[\pi_2^N].$$

Proof: Please see Appendix 3.

Proposition 3 shows some important implications. The value of information sharing to the manufacturer is intuitive. The rationale is that under information sharing, the manufacturer acting as leader has the e-retailer's forecast information, thus the manufacturer can benefit from the additional information to make an optimal wholesale pricing policy. Therefore, the manufacturer should actively cooperate with the e-retailer to pursue information sharing under any circumstances, even if the manufacturer needs to make some side payment to the e-retailer in order to motivate the e-retailer to share the forecasts. Our result in proposition 3 is consistent with results of prior study (Chiang and Feng, 2007).

However, our proposition 3 shows that the e-retailer's profit might decrease from information sharing. The rationale is that the manufacturer uses the information strategically to maximize its own profit. When $a_S < a_{rS}$ (the manufacturer's expectation of the e-retailer's forecast is higher than the e-retailer's actual forecast), the manufacturer overestimates the e-retailer's forecast and would like to set a higher

wholesale price in the non-information sharing setting. The e-retailer, in turn, then

will set a higher retail price resulting from higher charged wholesale price, which thus

leads to a decreased demand in the e-retailer. This will lead to decreased profits for

both the manufacturer and the e-retailer. Therefore, when the e-retailer shares

forecasts with manufacturer, the manufacturer's expectation of the retailer's forecast

reduces, which leads to reduced charge on the wholesale price. The e-retailer then

profits from the reduced wholesale price. Thus, when $a_S < a_{rS}$, the e-retailer always

would like to share its forecast with the manufacturer's one without any side payment.

However, when $a_S > a_{rS}$ (the manufacturer's expectation of the e-retailer's forecast is

lower than the e-retailer's actual forecast), the manufacturer will set a lower

wholesale price in the non-information sharing case. If the e-retailer shares its forecast

with the manufacturer's one, the manufacturer would like to charge a higher

wholesale price, which then in turn decreases the e-retailer profit.

Proposition 3 shows that the e-retailer would like to share forecast information

with the manufacturer only if $a_S < a_{rS}$ is satisfied.

3.5.1. Effect of e-retailer's market share on the value of information sharing

Furthermore, in order to examine the effect of e-retailer's market share on the

contribution of information sharing for each player, we differentiate

$\partial(E[\pi_i^S] - E[\pi_i^N])$ ($i = 1,2$) with respect to θ. $\dfrac{\partial(E[\pi_i^S] - E[\pi_i^N])}{\partial \theta}$ ($i = 1,2$) is the impact of a change in e-retailer's market share on the value of information sharing for each player. Therefore, from our analysis, we come up with proposition 4 as follows.

Proposition 4: *When $a_S < a_{rS}$, the value of information sharing for each player increases with the e-retailer's market share, θ.*

Proof. Proof is given in Appendix 4

Proposition 4 shows that when $a_S < a_{rS}$, both supply chain players (the manufacturer and the e-retailer) benefit more from the information sharing when the e-retailer's market share is larger. The rationale is intuitive that larger market share contributes more to profitability of firms, thus the information sharing is more valuable to the manufacturer and the e-retailer when θ is larger.

3.5.2. Effect of product's e-market base demand on the value of information sharing

To investigate how a product's e-market base demand affects the worth of information sharing for each player, we have derivative of $E[\pi_i^S] - E[\pi_i^N] (i = 1,2)$ with respect to $\bar{a}$ and obtain proposition 5.

Proposition 5: *When $a_S < a_{rS}$, the value of information sharing for each player increases with the product's e-market base demand, $\bar{a}$.*

Proof. Proof is given in Appendix 5

Intuitively, when the product is more compatible to e-market, its e-market base demand is larger. Thus proposition 5 shows the important implication that information sharing is more valuable to supply chain players when the product is more compatible with e-market.

3.6. Illustrative Simulation Examples

While our findings in propositions can be derived analytically, the analytical expressions are too complex to provide meaningful insights. Thus we now present simulation examples to illustrate the magnitude of manufacturer and e-retailer profits under the cases of non-information sharing and information sharing, and the impact of different model parameters, namely, $\theta, \bar{a}, \sigma_1$ and σ_2 on the profits of manufacturer and e-retailer as well as on the value of information sharing. In our simulation, we use the following parameter values: $b = 1$, $c = 10$, $\sigma_0 = 1$, $\rho = 0.1$. We vary the values of $\theta, \bar{a}$, σ_1, and σ_2 using the following data ranges.

$\theta \in \{0, 0.1, 0.2, 0.3, 0.4, 0.5, 0.6, 0.7, 0.8, 0.9, 1.0\}$

$\bar{a} \in \{100, 200, 300, 400, 500, 600, 700, 800, 900, 1000\}$

$\sigma_1 \in \{0, 1, 2, 3, 4, 5, 6, 7, 8, 9, 10\}$

$\sigma_2 \in \{0, 1, 2, 3, 4, 5, 6, 7, 8, 9, 10\}$

When each set of parameters analyzed, we assume that information sharing occurs only under the condition of $a_S < a_{rS}$.

3.6.1. Effect of e-retailer's market share, θ.

Insert in Figure 3.2 here

The impacts of the e-retailer's market share on the profits of the manufacturer and the e-retailer are shown in Figure 3.2. Since the manufacturer acts as the Stackelberg leader, its profit always is higher than the e-retailer's profit in this supply chain. Figure 3.2 shows that both the manufacturer and the e-retailer benefit from the

information sharing. Especially for the e-retailer, the information sharing is more

valuable (the gap between the information sharing curve and no information sharing

curve is larger) when the e-retailer's market share is larger.

3.6.2. Effect of product's e-market base demand, $\bar{a}$.

Insert in Figure 3.3 here

The impacts of product's e-market base demand on the profits of the

manufacturer and the e-retailer are shown in Figure 3.3. We saw in Figure 3.2 that the

manufacturer profit is higher than the e-retailer's profit and both the manufacturer and

the e-retailer benefit from the information sharing. These results hold in Figure 3.3 as

well and the reasons are the same. Furthermore, Figure 3.3 shows that to the e-retailer,

the value of information sharing is more valuable (the gap between the information

sharing curve and no information sharing curve is larger) when the product's e-market

base demand is larger.

3.6.3. Effect of manufacturer forecasting accuracy, σ_1.

Insert in Figure 3.4 here

The impacts of the manufacturer forecasting accuracy on each supply chain

player's profit are shown in Figure 3.4. The manufacturer's profit also is higher than

that of the e-retailer for all values of σ_1, the standard deviation of forecast error. The

reason is the same as in 3.6.1. In Figure 3.4, we also observe that the profits as well as

the value of information sharing (the difference between profits in the information

sharing case and non-information sharing case) increases for the manufacturer and the e-retailer as the forecast accuracy increases. This is to be expected because an improvement in forecast accuracy would reward both the cooperation of supply chain players. Particularly, the e-retailer can profit more from the information sharing.

3.6.4. Effect of e-retailer forecasting accuracy, σ_2.

Insert in Figure 3.5 here

Figure 3.5 summarizes the impacts of σ_2, the e-retailer forecasting accuracy, on the performance of each supply chain player. While the manufacturer and the e-retailer profits increases, the value of information sharing decreases for both the manufacturer and the e-retailer when σ_2 increases. The decline in the manufacturer and e-retailer profits when σ_2 increases, are to be expected because a higher σ_2 reduces the e-retailer's forecasting accuracy. Thus information sharing becomes less valuable for both the manufacturer and the e-retailer when the e-retailer's forecast becomes inaccurate.

3.7. Conclusions and Managerial Implications

In this research, we investigate the value of information sharing in a simple manufacturer-e-retailer supply chain. We show that information sharing has a strategic impact on the manufacturer and the e-retailer. While the manufacturer always benefits from the information sharing strategy, the e-retailer only can be better off when the manufacturer's forecast is sufficiently high. Thus information sharing may occur under some limited conditions. If the manufacture and e-retailer share the forecasts of information (when the manufacturer's forecast is sufficiently high), both can benefit from information sharing; especially, when the e-retailer's market share is larger and the product's e-market base demand is higher, they will profit more. Our simulation examples further show that information sharing is very valuable to both the manufacturer and the e-retailer when the manufacturer's forecast is sufficiently high. The e-retailer always benefits more from the information sharing when the accuracy of both the manufacturer and the e-retailer forecasts are high.

In today's business environment, retailers or individuals are increasingly using the Internet to sell directly to customers. The rise of this e-commerce phenomenon provides a motivation for retailers to better understand the sales and profit implications of this new system. Since the e-retailing is booming, it is managerially important to develop a mechanism of improving the accuracy of market information. This is an intuition based conclusion. In our paper, we use mathematical models to show that this intuition can be made objective by using an information sharing strategy. We prove that by strategically employing such a strategy, both the manufacturer and the e-retailer can effectively improve their individual profits, especially when the e-retailer's market share is larger and the product's e-market base demand is higher. This finding is of immense managerial significance since both the manufacturer and the e-retailer knowing that their profits would be enhanced, would feel the natural urge to improve the forecast accuracy by cooperative information sharing. Thus for example, Amazon, Overstock, and other larger market share e-retailers, they should actively pursue information sharing with the manufacturer, especially when the product category is more compatible with the e-retailing market

Figure 3.1: The information forecast diagram

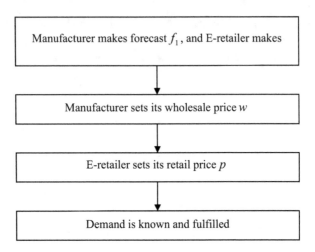

Figure 3.2: Impact of e-retailer's market share on supply chain players' profits

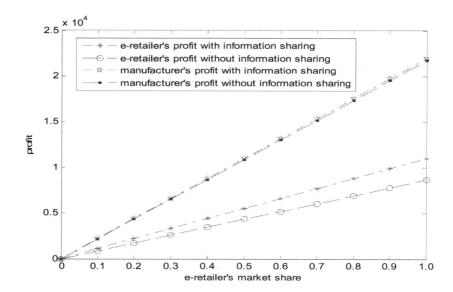

Figure 3.3: Impact of product's e-market base demand on supply chain players' profits

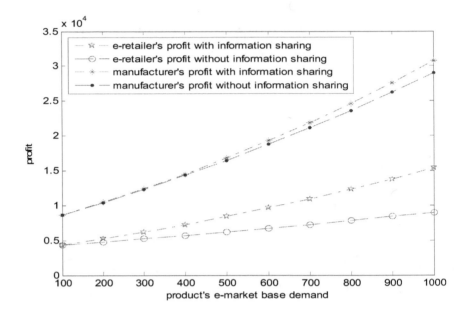

Figure 3.4: Impact of manufacturer's forecasting accuracy on supply chain players'

profits

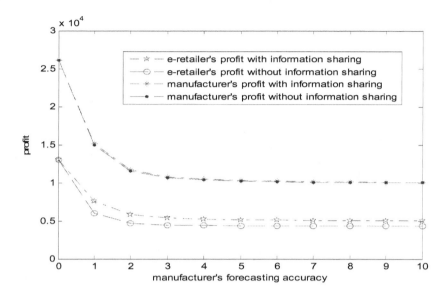

Figure 3.5: Impact of e-retailer's forecasting accuracy on supply chain players' profits

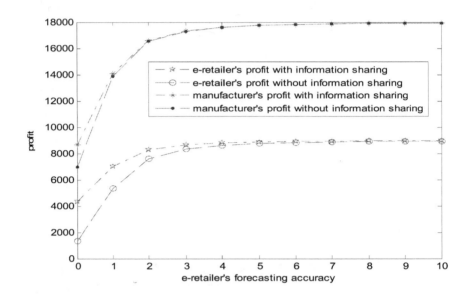

Appendix 1

When there is no information sharing between the manufacturer and the e-retailer,

$$E[\pi_1^N] = E[\theta(w-c)(a-bp) \mid f_1)]$$

$$E[\pi_2^N] = E[\theta(p-w)(a-bp) \mid f_2)]$$

And

$$E(a \mid f_i) = (1-t_i)\bar{a} + t_i f_i, \quad i = 1,2; \; j = 3-i \,,$$

$$E(f_j \mid f_i) = (1-d_i)\bar{a} + d_i f_i, \quad i = 1,2; \quad j = 3-i \,,$$

$$E(a \mid f_1, f_2) = I\bar{a} + Jf_1 + Kf_2 \,,$$

$$E[(f_i - \bar{a})^2] = E[(e + \varepsilon_i)^2] = \sigma_0 + \sigma_i, \quad i = 1,2$$

$$Var(a \mid f_i) = t_i \sigma_i^2, \quad i = 1,2$$

$$Var(a \mid f_1, f_2) = I\sigma_0^2$$

Where

$$t_i = \frac{\sigma_0^2}{\sigma_i^2 + \sigma_0^2} \,,$$

$$d_i = \frac{\sigma_0^2 + \rho\sigma_1\sigma_2}{\sigma_i^2 + \sigma_0^2}, i = 1,2.$$

$$0 \le \rho\sigma_1\sigma_2 \le \sigma_i^2$$

$$I = \frac{(1-\rho^2)\sigma_1^2\sigma_2^2}{(1-\rho^2)\sigma_1^2\sigma_2^2 + \sigma_0^2(\sigma_1^2 + \sigma_2^2 - 2\rho\sigma_1\sigma_2)}$$

$$J = \frac{\sigma_0^2(\sigma_2^2 - \rho\sigma_1\sigma_2)}{(1-\rho^2)\sigma_1^2\sigma_2^2 + \sigma_0^2(\sigma_1^2 + \sigma_2^2 - 2\rho\sigma_1\sigma_2)}$$

$$K = \frac{\sigma_0^2(\sigma_1^2 - \rho\sigma_1\sigma_2)}{(1-\rho^2)\sigma_1^2\sigma_2^2 + \sigma_0^2(\sigma_1^2 + \sigma_2^2 - 2\rho\sigma_1\sigma_2)}$$

In the Stackelberg game, we first find the e-retailer's pricing,

$$\frac{\partial (E[\pi_2^N])}{\partial p} = 0$$

Then we obtain

$$p = \frac{E(a \mid f_2) + bw}{2b}$$

Substituting $p = \dfrac{E(a \mid f_2) + bw}{2b}$ into $E[\pi_1^N] = E[\theta(w - c)(a - bp) \mid f_1)]$ and let

$$\frac{\partial (E[\pi_1^N])}{\partial w} = 0$$

After some computation, we then obtain all of the results summarized in proposition

1.

Appendix 2

When there is no information sharing between the manufacturer and the e-retailer,

$$E[\pi_1^S] = E[\theta(w - c)(a - bp) \mid f_1, f_2)]$$

$$E[\pi_2^S] = E[\theta(p - w)(a - bp) \mid f_1, f_2)]$$

Similarly, we find the e-retailer's price first,

$$\frac{\partial (E[\pi_2^S])}{\partial p} = 0$$

Then we obtain

$$p = \frac{E(a \mid f_1, f_2) + bw}{2b}$$

Substituting $p = \dfrac{E(a \mid f_1, f_2) + bw}{2b}$ into $E[\pi_2^S] = E[\theta(p - w)(a - bp) \mid f_1, f_2)]$ and

let

$$\frac{\partial(E[\pi_1^S])}{\partial w} = 0$$

After some computation, we then obtain all of the results summarized in proposition

2.

Appendix 3

Because

$$\pi_1^N = \frac{\theta(2a_S - a_{rS} - bc)(a_{rS} - bc)}{8b}$$

$$\pi_2^N = \frac{\theta(2a_S - a_{rS} - bc)^2}{16b}$$

$$\pi_1^S = \frac{\theta(a_S - bc)^2}{8b}$$

$$\pi_2^S = \frac{\theta(a_S - bc)^2}{16b}$$

Thus, $\pi_1^S - \pi_1^N = \dfrac{\theta(3a_S - a_{rS} - 2bc)(a_{rS} - a_S)}{16b}$

If $(a_{rS} - a_S)(3a_S - a_{rS} - 2bc) > 0$, $\pi_1^S - \pi_1^N = \dfrac{\theta(3a_S - a_{rS} - 2bc)(a_{rS} - a_S)}{16b} > 0$

and $\pi_2^S - \pi_2^N = \dfrac{\theta(a_S - a_{rS})^2}{8} > 0$

Therefore, proposition 3 is proved.

Appendix 4

When $(a_{rS} - a_S)(3a_S - a_{rS} - 2bc) > 0$

$$\pi_1^S - \pi_1^N = \frac{\theta(3a_S - a_{rS} - 2bc)(a_{rS} - a_S)}{16b} > 0$$

Thus, $\dfrac{\partial(\pi_1^S - \pi_1^N)}{\partial \theta} = \dfrac{(3a_S - a_{rS} - 2bc)(a_{rS} - a_S)}{16b} > 0$

And $\dfrac{\partial(\pi_2^S - \pi_2^N)}{\partial \theta} = \dfrac{(a_S - a_{rS})^2}{8} > 0$

Therefore, proposition 4 is proved.

Appendix 5

When $(a_{rS} - a_S)(3a_S - a_{rS} - 2bc) > 0$

$\pi_1^S - \pi_1^N = \dfrac{\theta(3a_S - a_{rS} - 2bc)(a_{rS} - a_S)}{16b} > 0$

Then, $\dfrac{\partial(\pi_1^S - \pi_1^N)}{\partial a} > 0$ and $\dfrac{\partial(\pi_2^S - \pi_2^N)}{\partial a} > 0$,

Therefore, proposition 5 is proved.

REFERENCES

Bakos, J.Y. (1997) "Reducing buyer search costs: Implications for electronic marketplaces", *Management Science*, Vol. 43, No.12, pp. 1679-1692

Balasubramanian, S. (1998) "Mail versus Mall: A strategic analysis of competition between direct marketers and conventional retailers", *Marketing Science*, Vol. 17, No. 3, pp. 181–195

Bassar,T. and Ho, Y.C. (1974) "Informational properties of the Nash solutions of two stochastic nonzero-sum games", *Journal of Economic Theory*, Vol. 7, pp. 370-387

Blattberg, R.C. and Hock, S.J. (1990) "Database models and managerial intuition: 50% model + 50% manager', *Management Science,* Vol. 36, No. 8, pp. 887-899

Brynjolfsson, E. and Smith, M.D. (2000) "Frictionless commerce? A comparison of Internet and conventional retailers", *Management Science*, Vol. 46, No. 4, pp.563-585

Cachon, G. and Fisher, M. (2000) 'Supply chain inventory management and the value of shared information', *Management Science,* 46, 8, 1032-1048

Cattani, K.D., Gilland, W.G. and Swaminathan, J.M. (2006) "Boiling frogs: Pricing strategies for a manufacturer adding a direct channel that competes with the traditional channel", *Production and Operations Management*, Vol. 15, No. 1, pp. 40-57.

Cheng, T. E. C. & Wu, Y. N. (2005). The impact of information sharing in a two-level supply chain with multiple retailers. The Journal of the Operational Research Society. Oxford, 56(10),   1159.

Chiang , W. K. & Feng, Y. (2007). The value of information sharing in the presence of supply uncertainty and demand volatility. International Journal of Production Research. London, 45(6), 1429.

Chiang, W. Y., Chhajed, D. & Hess, J. D. (2003). Direct Marketing, Indirect Profits: A Strategic Analysis of Dual-Channel Supply Chain Design. Management Science, 49(1), 20.

Corbett, C. J, Zhou, D. M and Tang, C. S. (2004) 'Designing supply contracts: contract type and information asymmetry', *Management Science,* 50, 4, 550-559

Cyert, R. M. and DeGroot, M. H. (1970) 'Bayesian analysis and duopoly theory', *Journal of Political Economics*, 78, 9, 1168-1184

Cyert, R. M. and DeGroot, M. H. (1973) 'An analysis of cooperation and learning in a duopoly context', *American Economics Review*, 63, 3, 24-37

Day, G. S. (1990) 'Market driven strategy: processes for creating value', *The Free Press*, New York

Gavirneni, S., Kapuscinski, R. and Tayur, S. (1999) 'Value of information in capacitated supply chains', *Management Science*, 45, 1, 16-24

Geyskens, I., Gielens, K. and Dekimpe, M.G. (2002) "The market valuation of Internet channel additions", *Journal of Marketing*, Vol. 66, pp. 102-119

Glazer, R. (1991) 'Marketing in an information-intensive environment: Strategic implications of knowledge as an asset', *Journal of Marketing*, 55, 10, 1-19

Hilton, R. W. (1981) 'The determinants of information value: synthesizing some general results', *Management Science*, 27, 1, 57-64

Hung, W., Chu, J., & Lee, C. C. (2006). Strategic information sharing in a supply chain. European Journal of Operational Research. Amsterdam, 174(3), 1567.

Johannes, L. (2000) "Competing online, drugstore chains virtually undersell themselves --- their web sites charge less than their own stores, with some strings attached", *Wall Street Journal*, (Jan 10, 2000) B1.

Kacen, J., Hess, J. and Chiang, W. K. (2002) 'Bricks or Clicks? Consumer Attitudes toward Traditional Stores and Online Stores', *working paper*, University of Illinois, Champaign, IL

King, R.C., Sen, R. and Xia, M. (2004) "Impact of Web-based e-commerce on channel strategy in retailing", *International Journal of Electronic Commerce*, Vol. 8, No. 3, pp. 103-130

Lee, H., So, V. K. and Tang, C. (2000) 'The value of information sharing in a two-level supply chain', *Management Science*, 46, 5, 626-643

Levary, R. and Mathieu, R.G. (2000) "Hybrid retail: integrating e-commerce and physical stores", *Industrial Management*, Vol. 42, No. 5, pp. 6-13

Liang, T. and Huang, J. (1998) 'An empirical study on consumer acceptance of products in electronic markets: a transaction cost model', *Decision Support Systems*, 24, 29-43

Li, S. H. & Lin, B.S. (2006). Accessing information sharing and information quality in supply chain management. Decision Support Systems. Amsterdam, 42(3), 1641.

McGee, J. and Prusak, L. (1993) 'Managing information strategically', *John Wiley*

Sons, Toronto, Ontario, Canada

Mishra, B. K. and Prasad, A. (2004) 'Centralized pricing versus delegating pricing to the saleforce under information asymmetry', *Marketing Science*, 23, 1, 21-27

Morrison, D. G. and Schmittlein, D. C. (1991) 'How many forecasters do you really have? Mahalanobis provides the intuition for the surprising Clemen and Winkler result', *Operation Research*, 39, 5, 519-523

Padmanabhan, V. and Rao, R. C. (1993) 'Warranty policy and extended service contracts: theory and application to automobiles', *Marketing Science,* 12, 6, 230-247

Raju, J.S. and Roy, A. (2000) 'Market information and firm performance', *Management Science*, 46, 8, 1075-1084

Rhee, B. and Park, S. (1999) "Online store as a new direct channel and emerging hybrid channel system", *Working paper,* Hong Kong University of Science and Technology, Clear Water Bay, Kowloon, Hong Kong

Sarvary, M. and Parker, P. M. (1997) 'Marketing information: a competitive analysis', *Marketing Science,* 16, 1, 24-38

Smith, M.D., Bailey, J. and Brynjolfsson, E. (2000) "Understanding digital markets: review and assessment", In understanding digital economy, E. Brynjolfsson and B. Kahin (eds.), Cambridge, MA: MIT Press.

Wigand R. and Benjamin R. (1995) "Electronic commerce: Effect on electronic markets", *Journal of Computer Mediated Communication*, Vol.1, No. 3

Vives, X. (984) 'Duopoly information equilibrium: Cournot and Bertrand', *Journal of Economic Theory,* 34, 71-94